WHY DO DOGS DO THAT?

Real Answers to the Curious Things Dogs Do

by Kim Thornton
illustrations by Keith Robinson

B⊠WTIE™
P R E S S
A Division of Fancy Publications

Library of Congress Catalog Card Number: 96-80216
ISBN: 1-889540-01-3

BowTie Press
3 Burroughs
Irvine, California 92618

Manufactured in the United States of America

First Printing January 1997

Second Printing Febuary 1998

Third Printing September 1999

10 9 8 7 6 5 4 3

Contents

Why Do Dogs Bark?

Well, if you couldn't talk, you would probably bark too. Dogs bark because they have something to say. Barking may sound like noise to us, but dogs can say a lot of things with their bark. "That guy in a blue uniform is attacking our front door again!" "A strange car has pulled into the driveway!" "Help! I've stuck my head through a hole in the fence and I can't get out." "Hey! You've been home for five minutes and you haven't said hello to me yet."

Dogs communicate with us in many ways, but barking is the loudest way they can get their point across. Dogs bark to warn us of danger and when they need help. Who can forget Lassie's warnings? "Bark! Bark!" (Translation: "Timmy's in the well!")

4

Dogs bark when they get excited, and sometimes they bark just for the fun of it. When you yell at them to stop, they get even more excited. "Cool! My owner's barking back at me. Now we can have a real conversation." To a dog, any kind of attention, even yelling, is something to celebrate.

Dogs have been barking for a long time. Back in the Stone Age, more than 10,000 years ago, wild dogs started hanging around people's caves, stealing their leftovers and trying to sneak in when it rained (much like dogs of today). These dogs taught their puppies how to mooch off people, and eventually the dogs lost their wildness, a process called domestication. One of the results of domestication is that dogs have kept many puppy-like characteristics, including barking. Adult wild dogs, such as wolves, coyotes, and foxes, bark very little, but their puppies bark a lot.

So that's why dogs bark. They are forever young, trapped in adolescence. And just like teenagers everywhere, they spend all their time talking to each other.

Why Do Dogs Chase Cars?

All day long, he tears off after the motorized monsters, barking and snapping at the tires. As each vehicle pulls away, the dog turns back with a satisfied expression. Score: Dog 5, Cars 0. Car-chasing is generally a territorial reaction, one that is often aimed at cars or trucks that drive by regularly, such as postal Jeeps or delivery vans.

Car-chasing can also be a form of predatory behavior, which is usually triggered by noise and motion. Predatory car-chasing is frequently engaged in by frustrated herding dogs. After all, the herding instinct is nothing but a redirected form of the prey drive, in which the dog circles and drives its prey but does not follow through with the kill. Such an ingrained behavior can be difficult to change, but it's not impossible.

As with most training, patience and consistency are the keys. If your dog chases particular vehicles (the neighbor's car or the mail carrier's Jeep), you can try a couple of methods. If the dog doesn't know the drivers, ask them to stop for an introduction. If the dog gets to know them, especially if they give him a treat, he will be less likely to view them—and their cars—as trespassers.

Other ways of curtailing the problem of car-chasing include regularly giving the dog more exercise away from his territory. Go for long walks or hikes, play a fast and furious game of Frisbee in the park, or go jogging on the beach.

These are the friendly methods. Should they fail, you may need to take more drastic and time-consuming steps.

9

Why Do Dogs Whine?

We've all heard the sound. High-pitched, it comes from the throat, enhanced by the sinuses, acting as resonance chambers. Depending on the situation, a whine could well be the most annoying sound a dog makes or the most awwww-inspiring.

Whining is perhaps one of the first sounds a young puppy makes. The pup's payoff? Warmth, food, comfort. He learns early on that a whine brings attention from Mom.

As they grow older, dogs learn that they can use this non-threatening noise to manipulate their people, too. Who can resist that combination of puppy-dog eyes and soft whimpering? Only the most hard-hearted of humans could refuse the whine that means, "Let's go for a waaaalk" or "I'm soooo hungry," especially when it is accompanied by that soulful glance that dogs do so well.

Some dogs whine when they're frightened. The sounds of fireworks or thunderstorms can bring on major whining attacks. When concerned owners rush to soothe their whining dogs, they reinforce the behavior, teaching the dog two things: one, that he has cause to whine, and two, that he's going to get attention for doing it. This encourages him to whine even more.

To nip whining in the bud, teach your dog that silence is golden. Ignore whining or other annoying sounds, and reward silence.

Why Do Dogs Wag Their Tails?

The TV show *Leave it to Beaver* could easily have featured a pack of dogs as its stars. (Can't you see a poodle playing the role of June; maybe a German shepherd as Ward? Wally and the Beav as puppies?) Canids, dogs and their wild cousins, live in social groups with family values that are actually much like our own. They communicate with sounds and with body language such as the tail wag. A wagging tail has a variety of meanings, depending on the position and speed of the tail. (We know that the tail wag is a means of communication because dogs wag their tails only at other dogs, people, or other animals—never at inanimate objects.)

The most familiar tail wag is a broad, medium-to-fast sweeping motion. Boy, is this dog happy to see you! She is showing the proper greeting given to the pack's top dog—in this case, you— indicating happiness and submission. The faster the tail, the more excited the dog.

Tail position can also telegraph interest, challenge, dominance, confidence, relaxation, fright, confusion, or aggression. A tail that is mostly horizontal but not stiff is usually attached to a dog who would like to find out more about you. She's interested but not yet challenging or aggressive. When the tail is fully horizontal, a challenge to either another dog or a person is in the offing. The dog who walks around with her tail up but not vertical says, "I'm top dog around here"; the dog who feels confident and in control holds her tail up and over her back.

A tail that is lowered but not between the legs usually belongs to a dog who is relaxed. A frightened or submissive dog tucks her tail between her legs. This is a universal signal in dogdom: "Please don't hurt me!" A dog whose tail wags slowly may be confused; she's not sure whether she should be making friends or on the attack. Watch out for dogs whose tails are bristling; their aggression is showing for all to see. A tail that is held high and stiff, wagging fast, is another telltale sign of a dog who shouldn't be messed with. An excited tail wag can be combined with aggressive signals at other areas of the body, so don't expect a wagging tail to be attached to a friendly dog all the time.

Who says dogs can't talk? Anyone who has studied the way a dog's tail wags knows that the canine vocabulary is pretty extensive. You just have to learn the language.

Why Do Dogs Hate the Mail Carrier?

I t's not just the uniform. Don't get the idea that dogs are rebels, growling at all forms of authority. Rather, it's due to the way your dog's brain is hardwired.

A dog's brain programs it to stake out and defend a territory. A typical canine territory contains a denlike area and its surroundings where the dog can hunt for food—in other words, your home and yard. Any "invasion" of this territory sets off alarm bells in the dog's head. "Gotta protect the home turf. Gotta keep the rest of the pack safe."

In the case of the mail carrier, this scenario is played out daily.

The mail carrier enters the yard and heads for the mailbox, the dog barks and growls, the mail carrier deposits the mail and leaves. Score: Dog 1, Mail carrier 0. That's how the dog sees it, anyway. In his mind, he has successfully driven off an intruder.

To put a stop to this behavior, introduce your dog to the mail carrier so they can get to know each other and become friends. Put your dog on a leash. When the mail carrier arrives, take the dog out to meet him or her. Be happy when you make the introduction. If your dog sees that you don't view the mail carrier as a threat, he will learn that he doesn't have to protect home and hearth against this specific "invader." Give the mail carrier a treat to give your dog. That should seal the friendship.

Why Do Dogs Lift Their Legs?

Sometimes you wonder if you're ever going to make it around the block. Your male dog stops every few feet to lift his leg—on trees, light poles, car tires. You name it, he'll mark it. You'd think he was leaving secret messages. In a sense, he is.

A dog's urine contains scent markers that delineate his territory, inform other dogs of his whereabouts, indicate his social standing and sexual availability, and warn off intruders. Dogs cock their legs to distribute scent at the highest point possible, allowing air currents to sweep it throughout the area.

That walk around the block every evening is like one long

continuous canine bulletin board. The urine marker left on an oak tree might say, "Bubba was here—male rottweiler, unneutered, likes to eat Special Beef Chunks, looking for a good time." On the grass beneath it is a reply: "Mimi calling—female bichon frise, in heat, eats only from Mamma's plate, hot to trot." Your dog thinks Mimi sounds pretty good—too good for Bubba—so he carefully aims a urine stream at Bubba's spot on the tree, hoping to cover it with his own message: "Lucky here—say, Mimi, wouldn't you like to get Lucky tonight?" You may notice, however, that dogs on common ground such as a park don't do as much leg-lifting. That's because they are all unsure of whose territory they are on, so they make an effort not to offend. Dogs who were not well socialized as pups may try to stake out territories on these neutral areas.

Leg-lifting behavior is okay outdoors on a walk, but it becomes a problem when the dog starts marking territory indoors. A dog left home alone may become nervous and lift his leg on furniture or walls to warn away potential intruders.

This dog may be suffering from separation anxiety. Accustom him to being home alone and reassure him that you will always return by leaving for only a few minutes and then returning. Gradually extend the amount of time you are gone until the dog is comfortable with being home alone. The dog may also benefit from staying in a dog crate.

Observers have found that dogs can urine mark up to 80 times in a four-hour period. A dog who frequently lifts his leg is expressing his dominant personality. Very dominant dogs may even urine mark other dogs or people. Leg-lifting is not limited to males. Very dominant females, especially among the terrier breeds, may also lift a leg.

Why Do Dogs Howl?

All canids, wild and domesticated, howl, and howls can have many meanings. Wolves have group howls before hunts, presumably to "psych themselves up" for the chase. A howl can communicate alarm or happiness. It says, "Honey, I'm home" or "Turn around and go back the way you came, stranger; this is my territory." Wolf packs howl to locate missing members, encourage stragglers on the trail, celebrate a successful hunt or the return of a pack member, or, in the case of loners, to find companionship. Each wolf has a distinctive voice identifiable by other wolves.

Our dogs howl for many of the same reasons. Dogs who are frequently left alone may howl a summons to their human pack: "Where are you? When are you coming back?"

Often, howling is a response to other howls. Dogs who howl at the sound of ambulance sirens may be responding to the siren's "howl." Beagles, bloodhounds, coonhounds and other scent hounds howl to indicate that they have located their quarry, whether it be a

raccoon, a lost child, or an escaped convict. This baying, or singing, of hounds, sometimes described as mountain music, allows hunters or handlers to locate their dogs. The comparison of howls to music is universal. As early as 1615, people used to combine hounds in a pack just to produce a symphony of sound. Many people report that their dogs howl along to the sound of music.

The dogs most likely to howl are hounds and northern breeds. Some people say their dogs howl when they are happy or sad or when the weather changes. Females in heat give come-hither howls.

So the next time your dog howls, you will know that he's communicating something important. With practice, maybe you can learn to understand what he's saying.

Why Do Dogs Sniff Butts?

There you are, talking to that really cute guy in the park, the one with the really cool Doberman, when your dog, not content with sniffing the Doberman's butt, decides to sniff the guy's butt, too. He gooses him a good one while you turn beet-red and yank on his leash, hissing at him to "stop that right now!"

Just think—if our noses had the sensitivity of a dog's, we'd probably be sniffing butts, too. Dogs and humans have individual scents, and that unnerving nose action is the canine version of an FBI check. The scents and secretions of the anus, genitals, and mouth tell a dog everything he needs to know, including whether the sniffee is male or female, its readiness for mating, social status, and what it likes to eat. Now, admit it: wouldn't it be handy to know all those things before you went out with someone?

Where a dog sniffs can say a lot. Friendly animals usually sniff each other's faces, heads, and necks, including inside the ears. Two dogs of equal rank will sniff each other's behinds at the same time. When a lower ranking dog encounters one that is more dominant, he waits submissively for the other dog to sniff under his tail.

Another dog doesn't have to be present for your dog to learn all about him or her. Sniffing urine and feces can also provide information. The special odors produced in a dog's urine and feces allow him to mark territory, leave warnings to trespassers, and attract sex partners.

If your dog is a little too socially aggressive with people, fight fire with fire. Instead of backing away (an action your dog might view as submissive behavior), move toward him, making him back away, and firmly tell him no. If he's sniffing someone else, divert his attention by making him sit or perform some other obedience command that will stop the unwanted behavior.

Why Do Dogs Chew?

A dog is an investigator at heart, the Sherlock Holmes of the animal kingdom. Her nose, ears, and eyes provide her with a huge amount of information. But to physically examine an object, a dog must use her mouth. After all, lacking an opposable thumb, her paws aren't much use at picking things up.

Chewing begins in puppyhood during the teething stage, which can last as long as a year. The chewing action helps relieve the pup's aching gums and builds strong jaw muscles and ligaments. Chewing is a natural canine behavior, but the problem with puppies is that they don't know what is okay to chew and what isn't. And think about it. If you were a dog, wouldn't you be attracted to the soft leather moccasins infused not only with the scents of the grocery store and the Grand Canyon but also with eau de Gloria Human?

   To start your puppy off on the proper sensory exploration track, provide her with appropriate chew toys and keep your shoes on your feet or behind closet doors. Encourage the puppy to examine her toys by making them taste and smell good. Smear hard rubber toys with bacon grease or chicken fat. Hollow rubber toys can be stuffed with peanut butter, soft cheese, or small smelly treats. Your dog will spend hours trying to get at the good stuff. For soft stuffed toys, use a scent your dog loves: you! Place the toy in your dirty clothes hamper for a few days so that it develops that familiar scent. But don't make the mistake of letting the dog chew your old, worn-out shoes or clothes. Chewbacca doesn't know the difference between holey sneakers and brand-new Nikes. Large sterilized knuckle bones or thigh bones are also acceptable, but avoid small bones or bones that splinter easily.

Once the teething stage is over, chewing doesn't necessarily stop. Dogs who are bored or anxious find chewing to be either a stimulating or a soothing activity. Chewing stimulates the dog's mind because she is learning about her surroundings, and it's a lot more interesting than just lying around all day. Chewing has a tranquilizing effect on dogs who miss their people, especially if they find something belonging to those people to chew on. If neither of these situations seems to be the problem, take your dog to the veterinarian for a checkup. Inflamed gums could be causing pain.

Prevention is always better than punishment. If your dog is a chronic chewer, put chewable items out of reach or confine her when you can't be around to supervise her. Coat chewable surfaces with a distasteful substance such as pepper sauce or Bitter Apple. If you find your dog **chewing on something inappropriate, distract her with a water squirter or shake can, then direct her attention to a chew toy. Most important, try to catch your dog in the act of chewing on the *right* thing. Reward her with a treat or praise when you do.**

Why Do Dogs Fetch?

The first job the first dog did for the first humans was to hunt. Caleb Flintstone (Fred's great-grandfather) was out hunting one day when he saw a pack of wolves off in the distance. They worked as a team to find their prey, surround it, and bring it down. "I could use some help like that," he thought to himself. The rest is history. But it wasn't until the mid-nineteenth century that modern hunters took the use of the dog one step further and taught it to find fallen game and bring it back, undamaged. The retriever is a specialist who can work on land or in water. Pointers, setters, and spaniels point or flush game but can also learn to retrieve.

Like so many behaviors, why the retriever retrieves can be

traced to its wild forebears. Wolves carry food back to the den for other pack members, especially puppies, so they can share in the feast. Retrieving ability is not limited to game, however.

No one who has seen a golden retriever endlessly fetch a tennis ball or Frisbee can doubt the dog's heritage. Today the retriever's desire to find and bring things, as well as its "soft mouth," make it indispensable as a service dog for people who are confined to wheelchairs.

Dogs such as retrievers have an amazing ability to plot trajectory (the path of a moving object) and predict its landing point on earth. If you doubt this, just watch a dog playing Frisbee.

So now you know that if you live with one of these retrieving fools, what you've really got on your hands is a canine rocket scientist.

Why Do Dogs Pounce on Their Toys?

Throw a toy for your puppy and watch her run after it. She pounces, takes the toy into her sharp little teeth, and shakes it wildly, growling all the while. "Kill the toy! Kill the toy!" you say with a laugh. And that's exactly what you're seeing: the killing instinct in action. Our dogs have millions of years of programming hardwired into their brains: chase, pounce, bite, eat.

Today, of course, most dogs have a more modern method of hunting: they wait patiently in the kitchen, staring up with big brown puppy-dog eyes, as their evening meal is plopped out of a can into a metal bowl. But instinct is not so easily put aside.

It has been said that a puppy's play is its work. The pouncing action, which is the consummation of the chase response, appears in puppies between four and five weeks of age. It is one of the behaviors that, through play, the puppy practices to become a successful dog. In the wild, it is believed that young wolves and coyotes who are old enough to hunt hone their play-practiced instincts by observing the adult members of the group.

Although the urge to track and kill prey is in most cases no longer necessary for canine survival, the behavior is innate. Since the dog has no prey upon which to practice, she uses the next best thing: her toys.

Why Do Dogs Pull on Their Leashes?

They were a sight. Twice a day, two boxers loped around the neighborhood, hauling a small woman behind them. She'd stumble by, barely able to get out a hello before being dragged ever onward. At last sight, she had taken up jogging so she could keep up with them.

Pulling can be related to either personality or heritage. Dominant dogs often are pullers. Pulling is also a behavior that is frequently seen in sled dog breeds such as Siberian huskies and Alaskan malamutes. It's understandable that sled dogs would be pullers—after all, that's what they were bred for. A sled dog with the personality of Winston Churchill—a commanding leader if ever there was one—is even more likely always to be out in front. But why do other breeds like to pull? Sometimes, it's part of their heritage, too. Bernese mountain dogs, Newfoundlands, Saint Bernards, and Great Pyrenees were all once used to pull carts for farmers or delivery people.

There are several things you can do to keep your dog from pulling on the leash. The first and easiest is to teach her while she's still a puppy not to pull. If she surges ahead, snap the leash and say no. Reward her for walking nicely beside you.

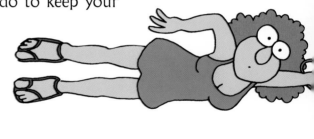

A dog who pulls because she wants to be the boss needs to learn her proper place in the family.

You can help reduce or stop the pulling behavior by taking the dominant position in the household. Never let this dog walk in front of you. Always walk through doors ahead of her, and feed her only after you have eaten.

A head collar, which is fashioned much like a horse halter, is a good way to control a dog who pulls. It is natural for a dog to pull against pressure, which is why so many dogs pull on their leashes. The head collar is designed to put pressure on the back of the neck, in much the same way that a dominant dog or mother dog imposes discipline, instead of the front of the throat. A head collar does not hurt the dog, and it is easy to use.

The most fun way to control a dog's tendency to pull is to redirect the instinct. Teach your dog to pull a small cart or wagon. Then she can help you unload the groceries or do yard work. If you live in a winter wonderland, you and your dog can take up skijoring, a sport in which your dog pulls you on skis, or dog-sledding. Mush!

Why Do Dogs Chase Cats?

For thousands of years, dogs and cats have been painted as enemies. Now, those of us who live in harmony with both cats and dogs know that they usually get along just fine. But as with most myths and misconceptions, there is a kernel of truth to the tale.

Both dogs and cats, wild and domesticated, are predators—mighty hunters of the natural world. Despite their long history of life as pets, the prey drive is often triggered by motion. This is especially true for sight hounds such as greyhounds or salukis; terriers, who were bred to go after furry vermin such as rats and moles; and sporting breeds, all of whom were bred for the hunt.

Even though dogs of these breeds may live in a city or suburb and never hunt, instinct kicks in when a cat (or squirrel or rabbit) flashes past. The quick movement attracts the dog's attention, inciting him to chase. For some dogs, all the fun is in the chase. In others, however, the prey drive is so powerful that

the dog carries it through to its logical conclusion: the death of the animal being chased—if it is caught. This is especially common in breeds that have a strong hunting instinct but no outlet for their innate behavior.

Sometimes, dogs seem to differentiate between cats in the house (off limits) and cats outside (fair game). How the cat reacts is important, too. A cat who stands his ground and hisses or swipes at the dog is far more likely to escape with his life than one who runs. Faced with a spitting, scratching cat, the smart dog will often turn tail and run.

We all know from experience that it's difficult to change a habit—especially a bad one—and changing the instinctive habit of a dog is equally difficult, but can sometimes be done. Patience, consistency, and sometimes the help of a trainer or behaviorist are necessary.

If your dog loves to chase cats, there are some things you can try to put the brakes on his bad habit. Keep the dog on leash, even in the house if necessary, until the situation is under control. When Speedy tries to go after a cat, redirect his attention to a favorite ball or toy. Playtime with the special ball should be limited to when cats are around.

Sometimes, the substitution of a toy isn't enough. If your dog continues to try to chase cats, give him a leash correction or use an unpleasant sound to break his concentration. When his attention is focused on you instead of the cat, reward him with a treat or toy. Your dog must learn that running after cats equals trouble; ignoring them brings good things. Never let your dog stare intently at a cat, either; again, correct him by saying no or using unpleasant noise.

Why Do Dogs Eat Grass?

Grass is the last thing we would expect a member of the order Carnivora to eat, yet eating grass is one of the most common behaviors of dogs. They nibble delicately, grazing the yard as if they were goats. Then they go inside and throw up on the Oriental rug that great-aunt Clara brought back from Iran when it was still called Persia.

It's often a matter of great concern to dog owners when their pets eat grass. They take their dogs to the veterinarian, write to dog magazines for advice, and ask all their friends what they think is the matter. The fact is, however, that eating grass is a pretty harmless activity. As far as we can tell, dogs do it just because they like it.

Eating grass may also fulfill an instinctive need for greenery in the diet. Wild dogs eat every part of their usually herbivorous prey, including the grassy contents of their stomachs. It could be that grass provides fiber or certain vitamins and minerals not found in meat. And not all dogs throw up after eating grass. Some dogs seem to enjoy it as a regular part of their diet. If your dog enjoys eating grass, consider growing a small planter of grass for her, since grass outdoors may be treated with pesticides or infested with parasite eggs.

NKR

Why Do Dogs Dig?

Dogged digging is a basic part of the canine lifestyle. A nice, comfy hole makes a great bed. Dogs around the world have known this for millennia. In the great white north, ancestors of Alaskan malamutes and Siberian huskies dug holes in the snow, where they curled up with their tails over their noses to keep warm. Today, malamutes and huskies are still known as mighty diggers, but now their living conditions have changed. Bred for cooler climes, the California malamute or Florida husky is likely to dig in the dirt to form a cool bed, especially during hot summers.

Other reasons dogs dig are for protection, storage, prey, and entertainment. Wild dogs dig dens to protect their young from storms and predators. Canines use holes as pantries or refrigerators. They catch and eat a big meal, dig a hole, and bury the leftovers for later. Of course, the next time they're hungry, they have to dig out their doggie bag.

Some breeds, notably terriers, were bred to dig. That's how they find their prey, tough tunnel- or den-dwelling creatures such

as badgers, moles, and foxes. These types of terriers with short, strong legs, among them cairn terriers, rat terriers, Scottish terriers, and Skye terriers, are built for digging.

Finally, just like humans, some dogs dig for entertainment. The scent of turned earth is fresh and exciting to a dog, whose nose is much more highly developed than our own. What could be down there? The possibilities are endless! And digging is fun, especially when the dirt goes flying.

The brighter and more bored the dog, the more likely she is to dig. After all, excavation and construction are intense, time-consuming activities. (Dogs would probably make pretty good paleontologists.) A dog stuck alone in a backyard has to do something to pass the time.

If your dog has gone from being a bull-terrier to a bulldozer, there are several things you can try to solve the problem. If it's too hot outside, relocate Digger to a cooler area—a shaded part of the yard or inside the house. When you catch her in the act of digging, firmly say no and then distract her with a toy or game. Houdini dogs, those who dig to escape the yard, require a little more effort. You may need to place a concrete or wire barrier beneath the fence to keep them confined. With a hard-core hole digger, who digs purely for the fun of it, you may have to compromise a little. Try setting aside an area of the yard where it's okay for your dog to dig. Spike the area with treats and toys to make it attractive. But the only foolproof way to prevent digging is to supervise your dog whenever she is in the yard. Attention is the best antidote to boredom.

Why Do Dogs Roll in Dead Fish?

No one really knows why dogs like to coat themselves in what to us are disgusting smells, but theories abound. For a dog, rolling in dead fish or other stinky substances may be akin to the human purchase of a Hawaiian shirt or a red silk teddy from Victoria's Secret. It makes them stand out from the crowd or even seem more attractive to the opposite sex. To look at it another way, the canine appreciation of foul odors can be compared to a cheese lover's appreciation of a ripe Limburger or Liederkranz cheese.

Another possibility is that the practice may serve as

camouflage. Just as soldiers paint their faces and wear clothing designed to blend into their surroundings, dogs may "wear" certain odors to hide their scent from predators or prey.

Some people who study dogs think that smelly fur may be another way dogs communicate. It allows them to say, "This is what I found when I was out hunting."

It's safe to say that this is one of those questions to which we will never have a really good answer, except to say that it's in**stink**tive.

Why Do Dogs Jump on People?

Susie: "Sparky, I'm so happy to see you! What a good dog you are! I missed you so much today! That's right; jump up here and see me!"

Sparky: "Susie, my slave-companion, it's about time you got home. Just wait until I jump up and show you how much more important I am than you."

Susie would no doubt be surprised to learn that Sparky's body slam was an attempt at dominance rather than a loving greeting. Jumping up is one of the most misunderstood dog behaviors, and it is one that people encourage from earliest puppyhood. A puppy who jumps up is pretty darn cute, but by the time Sparky weighs 125 pounds, his jumping isn't so cute anymore.

Like most behaviors, jumping is common to all dogs, wild and domesticated. It begins in puppyhood as a desire for food or sign of submission. Wolf pups jump up on their mother after she returns from a hunt, licking her lips to induce her to regurgitate food for them—instant baby food, if you will. The lip-licking behavior is also a sign of submission: "I'm sorry I was too rough when I jumped on you, Ma; please forgive me."

In adulthood, however, the jumping behavior evolves into an attempt at dominance. The taller a dog stands, the more status he has. If he can stand over or jump on a rival, he has the upper paw, so to speak. The same motivation is seen in dogs. What you may view as a sign of greeting or affection may have a very different interpretation by your dog, especially if he is large or aggressive. In some cases, the attempt to push away such a dog can have serious consequences.

To stop jumping in its tracks, it's best to begin when the dog is young and easier to control, but a dog of any age can learn to give a proper welcome. Start by always greeting your dog calmly. Come in the door, put away your things, and then greet the dog in a room away from the front door. If your dog tries to jump, turn aside and ignore him. Don't yell or try to knee him. Dogs will work for any kind of attention, positive or negative, but they hate being ignored. You can replace the jumping behavior by teaching your dog to sit when you arrive. Reward the sit with a treat or praise.

Why Do Dogs Cock Their Heads?

What would we do without dogs? They sit with head cocked, listening attentively as we pour out our woes or joys. They must understand every word we say.

Well, not necessarily, but dogs definitely hear every word we say, whether they respond or not. A dog has an incredible sense of hearing compared to our own.

At low frequencies, dog and human hearing is similar, but dogs have us beat when it comes to hearing high-frequency sounds. Sharp ears are a must for predators such as dogs, allowing them to hear prey animals who often communicate

with high-frequency sounds.

But it's not just the dog's ability to hear that is so interesting.

It's how he does it. By orienting his head in the direction of a sound and manipulating his ears, a dog can detect the source of a sound in as little as six-hundredths of a second. Canine ears act as antennae. The pinna—the external ear flap—is mobile, allowing the ears to be pointed in different directions or in the same direction. It's not for nothing that a dog with a cocked head was featured in the RCA Victrola ads.

Ear position is also a means of communication. When a dog's ears go forward, it's usually in response to sound or a new situation. This dog is indicating great interest; he wants to know what's going on. Because dogs are pack animals, who must pay close attention to sounds and body language to get along, listening is important to them in a social context. That's why dogs listen so intently to us and why they so often seem to read our minds. Their hearing ability and observational skills allow them to interpret certain tones of voice and even to learn how to spell. Doesn't your dog know what w-a-l-k or c-o-o-k-i-e means?

Despite their auricular talents, dogs are known to have selective hearing. So the next time you call Sounder and he doesn't respond, you'll know he's either going deaf or is choosing to ignore you. To test his hearing, try whispering his name or rattling a box of treats to get his attention.

Why Do Dogs Eat Poop?

Dogs aren't finicky. No social mores holding them back, no sirree! Those of us who live with them know that given half a chance, most dogs will eat anything: vomit, rotting road kill, and, most disgusting of all, feces—either their own or from another animal.

In some instances, eating poop is not an entirely unnatural behavior. Mother dogs lick the anal areas of their newborn puppies to stimulate elimination. Then they swallow the resulting feces and urine to keep the nest area clean until the puppies are old enough to learn not to soil it. In the wild, this habit also makes the area less likely to attract predators. Nor is it unusual for pups to eat their mother's feces, which can provide some nutrition.

But in adult dogs, eating poop is not a normal behavior. In many cases, its cause is believed to be that most common of culprits: boredom. Dogs who lack interesting toys, regular human companionship, or a change in scenery or activity may turn to poop eating for want of anything else to do. They may eat their own feces or the feces of other animals. Some dogs especially like snacking out of the cat litter box. Maybe they think they're getting Tootsie Rolls.

As unappetizing as it may seem, eating poop is not necessarily a harmful practice, although in some cases it can cause parasite infestation. And, of course, face licking is out of the question.

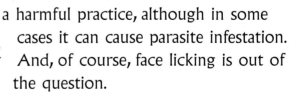

There is only one surefire way to stop your dog from eating poop: prevention. Walk your dog on a

If your dog has developed this practice, try livening up her routine. Regular exercise and toy rotation may add some interest to her life. Feeding more than one meal a day is another way to relieve boredom. It's always a good idea to schedule a veterinary exam for a dog who eats feces. It may be that a parasite infestation is causing the dog to have a ravenous appetite, leading her to eat anything she can find. Your dog may have a nutritional deficiency.

Discuss your dog's diet with your veterinarian, and ask about providing the dog with vitamin B supplements. Sometimes a change in diet—to a food that is higher in fiber, fat, or protein—solves the problem.

leash so you can pick up after her immediately. Put the cat's litter box in an area that is inaccessible to the dog. Muzzle the dog when you can't supervise her in the yard. Other options include teaching a don't touch command or adding pancreatic enzymes (found in some commercial products) to food to make the feces taste bad.

Why Do Dogs Stick Their Heads Out of Car Windows?

It's a classic image: a dog with his head stuck out the car window, ears flying, tongue hanging out. Why? Until now, no one has known. But after arduous research, the top 10 reasons dogs like to stick their heads out of car windows have been discovered.

10. So they can smell what's going on around them

9. So they can check out the beautiful bitch in the Jaguar two lanes over

8. Because they like to feel the wind ruffling their fur

7. Because the view is better

6. In case they get carsick and have to vomit

5. So they can howl along with the horns and sirens

4. So the wind can blow the slobber off their mouths

3. So they can grab any food that might be flying by

2. They're hoping the fresh air will clear away the smell of that rottweiler's butt

1. Because dogs just wanna have fun

Now that that's settled, the next question is: should you let your dog stick his head out the car window? The answer: probably not. Remember what your mother always said about sticking your arm out the car window? It's going to get torn off by a passing car, right? Well, not only do you have to worry about that happening to your dog's head, there's also the more likely possibility that flying debris could injure his eyes. But if you just can't bring yourself to deny Snoopy the pleasure of the wind blowing through his fur, try fitting him with goggles to protect those puppy-dog eyes. He'll be the coolest dog on the road.

Dogs have been our friends for thousands of years, so they know us pretty well. Now that we know them a little better, we can look forward to an even closer friendship.

For more authoritative and fun facts about dogs, including health-care advice, grooming tips, training advice, and insights into the special joys and overcoming the unique problems of dog ownership, go to your local pet shop, bookstore, or newsstand and pick up your copy of *Dog Fancy* magazine today.

BowTie™ Press is a division of Fancy Publications, which is the world's largest publisher of pet magazines. For further information on your favorite pets, look for DogsUSA®, CatFancy®, CatsUSA®, BirdTalk®, Horse Illustrated®, Reptiles®, Aquarium Fish®, Rabbits®, FerretsUSA™, and many more.